COPYRIGHT

CW01431204

DISCLAIMER

ABOUT THE AUTHOR

Ryan J. Mathias

Hi,

I'm Ryan Mathias, creator of the Mathias Method Strength System and for years I have been helping people all over the world, from total beginners to elite athletes, learn how to get stronger, perform better, and achieve their goals.

As an athlete, Strength Coach and competitive Powerlifter with 10+ years of experience, all backed by a Degree in Exercise Science, I have taken my experience and combined it with my education to bring you the best and most effective knowledge available.

I share everything I know in my books and it is my goal to help as many people as I can learn how to achieve their goals. Because I measure my success not by how many books I sell, but by how many people I help.

So, if you want to learn how to get bigger, stronger, faster, and overall perform better, then I'm your guy!

Plus, if you ever have any questions, you can email me anytime and I will do my best to help you reach your goals!

Email: ryan@mathiasmethod.com
I would love to hear from you!

Join me on Social Media: @RyanJMathias

BOOKS BY RYAN J. MATHIAS

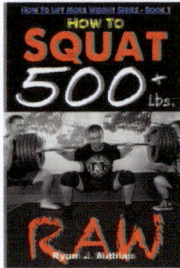

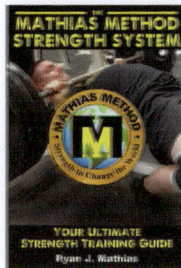

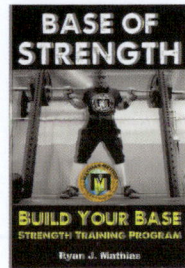

Available on

Amazon.com

and

StrengthWorld.store

TABLE OF CONTENTS

FULL POWER
POWERLIFTING PROGRAM

Reach Your Full Strength Potential!

This Program is based on the Mathias Method Strength System.

This is a 16-Week FULL POWER Powerlifting Program. It is the exact Powerlifting Program my team of Strength Warriors and I have used for years leading up to all of our Powerlifting Meets. It has worked really well and given us a lot of success. So we want to share that success with you!

To be honest, it is really hard. It has a lot of sets, a lot of reps, and a lot of work. But, if you can get through it, this program will make you brutally strong! *I guarantee it!*

PROGRAM DETAILS

This is a 4-day per week, 16-Week Powerlifting Program that is designed to increasing your squat, bench press and deadlift strength all at once. In it I will guide you through the exact work you need to do in order to reach your new Max Strength in all 3 lifts!

Also, this program is meant to be used to repeatedly, as you continuously improve your lifts over and over again. After you finish one 16-week cycle, simply take a week to recover, if needed, then begin again!

For many, this program may seem like a lot, but to lift more weight than you ever have before, you have to put in more work than you ever have before. You have to do hard things, because hard things make you stronger.

THIS PROGRAM HAS 3 PHASES:

1. **Volume Phase** (4-Weeks)

2. **Strength Phase** (8-Weeks)

3. **Max Phase** (4-Weeks)

If needed, you can trim off the Volume Phase, and even a few weeks of the Strength Phase, to accommodate specific Powerlifting Meet dates. But the more of the programs that you do, the better your results. Just make sure that you DO NOT change any of the Max Phase, including the deload week.

Note: This program is best for lifters with at least a year of lifting experience under their belt. If you have not been practicing your lifts for that long or more, then you will benefit more from my Base Of Strength Training Program (see page 4), which is made to give you a strong base to build on before going for maximal strength.

PHASE 1 - VOLUME

The first 4-weeks of your training is the Volume Phase. This Phase will focus on increasing your total work capacity with light to moderate weight and a lot of volume.

This is the time to improve your technique and reset your lifts so that your body is ready for the more intense work ahead without getting over-fatigued.

This Volume Work is also used as a "Strength Reset" in which you give your body time off from maximal work to prepare it for more progress at your new found strength. This Phase is vital for your maximal strength, and will have your body craving more intense weights when complete.

DO NOT do any Daily Max overload sets during this phase! Let your body rest from maximal work. Instead, stick to AMRAP (As Many Reps As Possible) sets, as is prescribed.

PHASE 2 - STRENGTH

The next 8-weeks (5-12) is the Strength Phase. These workouts combine intensity and volume to build up the greatest amount of strength.

They will be long and hard, but you will feel like a true Strength Warrior if you can get through them without being crushed by the weight!

Take your time with every set and make sure that you are moving with a purpose on every rep. Be in control of the weight, and do not let the weight take control of you.

DELOAD WEEK

Week 13 in this program is a deload and recovery week. This week allows your body to catch up on recovery, build up other weak areas and prepare you for the Max Phase.

This is the time to focus on your accessory lifts, that will help to build up your body's weak areas and improve your overall strength.

During this week's training, your Main Lifts (Squat, Bench, Deadlift) can stay the same or be a close variation to build up your weak points.

For Squats, if you have weak quads you should do close stance squats or front squats. If you have weak hips or hamstrings, then do wide stance squats or box squats.

For Bench Press, if you have weak triceps you should do closegrip bench press or floor press. If you have weak shoulders and chest, then do incline bench press or dumbbell press.

For Deadlifts, do 1-2" deficit deadlifts using a conventional stance, whether you normally do Sumo or Conventional.

The intensity will be much lower on this week and you should not push yourself too hard. Just get in some work to improve your lift, but save most of your energy for the intense workout the following week.

DO NOT do any Daily Max Overload sets this week! Only AMRAP sets, as is prescribed.

PHASE 3 - MAX

The final 4-weeks (13-16), including your deload week, are what is called your Max Phase, or Peaking Phase. These workouts are designed to increase your maximal strength and prepare you to crush your Peak Week!

This is where you have your most intense workouts before backing off for at least 7-10 days in order to hit a Strength Peak where your body is ready to lift the most weight for all 3 of your lifts.

These 4-weeks are crucial to nail perfectly in order to peak at the right time and get the greatest improvement in your lifts.

Make sure your recovery is on point and you do not do anything out of the ordinary during these 4-weeks.

PEAK WEEK

Peak Week is the last 7-10 days before your Meet Day, and starts after your Week 15 - Workout 2 Strength Work is complete.

To set up for your strength peak, you will start your Weeks 14 (Deadlift) and 15 (Squat and Bench Press) Strength Workouts by working up to the heaviest weight that you feel you can do 2-3 clean reps with, but only do singles with it. This is likely around 90-95%, of your previous max at the start of the program, but can also be well over your previous 100% max, depending on how well the program has worked for you so far.

When you find your working weight you are going to do 5-10 singles with it, stopping when form begins to break down too much. If form breaks down before you reach 5 reps, then you need to significantly drop the weight to where you can do clean singles. If you are working into a competition, then this working weight should be your opening lift.

DO NOT go for a Max during these workouts! Use the same weight for all sets.

This workout should give you a good idea of what your max should be on Meet Day. If this workout goes well, then you can expect to hit 110%+ of this weight on Meet Day. For example, if you were able to do 5-10 good singles with 450 lbs. then you can expect to do 500+ lbs. on Meet Day. That makes 500 lbs your Projected Max.

These are your last strength workouts before your Meet Day and you should plan to max 7-10 days after your Week 15 - Workout 2.

You will finish Week 15 off with your normal Base Work before moving to week 16.

Week 16 is also a deload week in which you will do minimal work and very low intensity for all of your lifts, so that your body is more than ready for Meet Day.

You will start the week by doing very light weight lifting just to practice the movements and improve recovery, followed by your normal Accessory Work. Keep your accessory work light and easy on these days and just get some movement in. You do not want to take the week off from lifting, but you also do not want to fatigue yourself with any of your workouts.

Keep all your workouts light and easy this week and have at least 2-3 days off from all training before Meet Day.

IT'S ALL FOCUSED ON MEET DAY

Your set-up, how you perform each lift, along with everything else in this 16-Week FULL POWER Powerlifting Program, is focused upon obtaining the most strength for Week 16.

Week 16 is your competition week and there should be no lifting done during the last 2-3 days leading up to your Meet Day. Do your training early in the week with little accessory work so that you are fully recovered before the meet.

When it's time, be smart, but go BIG! Open with a weight you know you can get, even on a bad day. Base your second attempt on how that felt/moved, and choose something you know you can get. Then, on the third attempt, let the demons out and show the world what you're made of!

MEET DAY

Meet Day is your day. It is the day you have prepared for with every workout over the past 16-Weeks. You are ready for this and you should wake up feeling super human!

Make sure that you are fully rested on the days leading up to your Meet Day and your nutrition is on point.

Stay hydrated and eat normally. Do not try any new supplements or food protocols around this day. You don't need to be overly stuffed or caffeinated to lift heavy. You have been preparing for weeks and you are ready. Just go do it.

Be prepared. Wake up on time, check that you have everything you need, and get to the meet early.

Start warming up early with plenty of time before your flight. As you get over 80% with your lifts, your rest should be 5-10 minutes between sets.

Make sure everything is feeling good and move violently. If the weight is light, then it should look light. Drive into every rep as if it is your max and make sure your body is prepared to be explosive.

If you prepared properly, then this day will be easy for you.

When you are ready, go for it! Be confident in yourself and show the world WHO YOU ARE!!! It's Game Time! Go dominate!

Also, remember to tag @MathiasMethod when you post your meet PRs so I can see how you did!

If you want some good Game Day Motivation, then check out my motivational book *Motivated Mindset*! It will get you fired up for anything you pursue in your life no matter the challenges you face!

On Meet Day, how you work up to your attempts can greatly effect your maximal strength. The goal is to stimulate your body for a maximal lift without over-fatiguing yourself to where you have major strength loss.

If you go in and do a bunch of unnecessary reps you are just going to be waisting energy. It is better to do more sets and less reps to conserve energy than try to do a full workout before hand. You wouldn't run a mile to warm up for a sprint, so don't make the same mistake here. All you need to do is feel the weight. When the weight feels good, move up.

Start with your normal stretching/bodyweight warm-up routine. If you don't have one, you can follow my *How To Warm-Up Properly For Strength Training Guide* (see page 4).

When you start lifting, take your time between warm-up sets and go when you are ready keeping the reps low. Remember, the goal is to get your body prepared for maximal weight, not fatigue you. Always be explosive with every single rep as if it is a maximal lift.

- **Opener:** Your opener, or first attempt, should be something you know you can do with perfect competition style form. This weight was determined on your last heavy Strength Workout for each Main Lift and is likely 90-95% of your projected maximum.

- **2nd Attempt:** Your second attempt is based on how your first attempt went. If it was easy, take a reasonably large jump of 5-7%. If it was hard, to take a small jump of just 3-5% or less.

- **3rd Attempt:** Your third attempt should be the heaviest weight you believe you can do, based on how your 2nd attempt went. Be honest, but also push yourself. This is the lift that can change your world. So make it happen!

- **Redo any missed lifts, unless it was due to technical error.** If it was due to technical error, you can redo the same weight or take a small jump, as long as it is something you can easily correct.

- **Bar x 5-10**

- **30-40% x 5-10**

- **50-60% x 3-5**

- **70-75% x 3**

- **80-85% x 1-3**

- **90-95% x 1** (Opener)

- **100-105% x 1** (2nd Attempt)

- **105%+ x 1** (3rd Attempt)

Add multiple sets as needed.

All percentages are based on your projected max calculated by your last Heavy Strength Workout's working weight multiplied by 110%. For example, if you used 450 lbs. as your working weight for all 5-10 singles, then your projected max is 500 lbs.

If you had to lower the weight for that workout, then use the lower weight to calculate your projected max.

It is better to warm-up a little lighter than it is to warm-up going too heavy.

WEEKLY WORKOUT SCHEDULE

This FULL POWER Powerlifting Program has you lifting 4 times per week. Workouts 1 and 2 are your Strength Work in which you will be improving your maximal strength through intense training. Workouts 3 and 4 are your Base Work in which you will be practicing your technique, strengthening your weaknesses, and increasing your overall training volume.

Your first workout of the week is the heaviest and hardest. So, make sure that you have at least 1 rest day before this training session, in which you do no gym or cardio work. That will allow you to be fresh and prepared to take on the challenging workout ahead.

The second workout of the week is similar and should also have a rest day before and after it, if you can work it in. If not, it would be best to at least have a rest day after.

Your Base Work can be moved around as needed, as these workouts are easier and meant to improve recovery, but it is very important to include a rest day between Workout 4 and Workout 1 of the next week.

This is the training split we have found most effective for this program.

Day 1 - **Workout 1** (Squat/Deadlift Strength Work)

Day 2 - Off

Day 3 - **Workout 2** (Bench Press Strength Work)

Day 4 - Off

Day 5 - **Workout 3** (Squat/Deadlift Base Work)

Day 6 - **Workout 4** (Bench Press Base Work)

Day 7 - Off

WORKOUTS

STRENGTH WORK

The first two workouts of each week are your "Strength Work" in which you will focus on building maximal strength. These workouts will have the heaviest lifts of the training week and require the most preparation and recovery.

The first 4-weeks of Strength Work are moderate intensity and volume workouts to increase your work capacity and prepare for the high demanding workload ahead. These workouts will each include an AMRAP for your last set to push your main lift's volume tolerance.

The following 8-weeks will gradually increase in intensity to build strength as you work towards peak week. These workouts will include a daily max for your main lifts after your main sets. This is where you will be able to work up to a heavy 1-3 rep fatigued max to increase your maximal strength.

Week 13 is a deload week in which you will take a break from the intense lifting and work on other lift variations. This is the time where you can do a simple variation of your main lift and work on a weak area.

Peak week is the last 7-10 days before your maximal lift attempt, starting after your Week 15 - Workout 2 (Bench Work). It is crucial that you do this properly to get maximum results.

For your Strength Work on Weeks 14 (Deadlift) and 15 (Squat and Bench Press) you will work up to the heaviest weight you feel that you can do for about 2-3 reps, but make sure that you only do 1 rep. This is likely around 90-95%, of your previous max at the start of the program, but can also be well over your previous 100% max, depending on how well the program has worked for you so far. You are going to do 5-10 perfect singles with this weight, stopping only when you cannot perform the lift with reasonable form. Be careful not to push yourself too hard in this workout. You want to work hard, but not get injured before your max day.

After doing 5 or more singles with this weight, you can add a little weight, but no more than 3-5% if you feel good. If it is getting heavy during your first 5 singles, then maintain the same weight until form breaks down. DO NOT go for a max during these weeks. Save some for your meet.

Week 16 is your official peak week in which you use very light weight and just work on the movement. You want to stretch out the movement, and allow for blood flow, but focus on recovery above all else.

Your Meet should be 3-5 days after your workout(s) this week. Make sure that you get plenty of rest this week and are prepared for Meet Day!

BASE WORK

The last two workouts of each week are your Base Work. These are light to moderately intense workouts to help you get in more work while improving your technique.

For your Base Work you will be doing at least 5 sets of 5 reps with gradually increasing intensity. Most of the time you will be given a 5% range to work in. For this, work up to a weight within the range that feels good and moves well.

How you feel during these workouts will vary every week, so do not worry so much about the weight, even if you have to go lighter than expected. It is more important to focus on moving well and with perfect technique. Save the heavy stuff for your Strength Work days. Think of it as a movement and recovery workout.

As for your technique, since the weights are lighter for these workouts, every rep should be explosive and done with perfect form. Do not take it easy just because it is light. If it is light, then you should make it look easy by driving the weight up hard with every rep.

Also, for these workouts, only use equipment (belt, sleeves, wraps, etc.) if needed. Try to do every set 100% RAW, if you can. This will help increase your RAW strength and make you that much stronger when you do use equipment on other days.

Week 16 you will not have any Base Work as you prepare for Meet Day. Use this as a recovery period.

Note: There are no Deadlifts for the first 3 weeks of Base Work due to high squat volume.

PROGRAM CHART

STRENGTH WORK

WEEK	MAIN LIFTS	SETS	REPS	% MAX
	— Workout 1 —			
1	Deadlift	5	5	70%
	Squat Variation	4	8	40-45%
	— Workout 2 —			
	Bench Press	5	5	65%
	— Workout 1 —			
2	Squat	5	5	70%
	Deadlift	4	6	55-60%
	— Workout 2 —			
	Bench Press	5	5	70%
	— Workout 1 —			
3	Deadlift	5	5	75%
	Squat Variation	4	8	40-45%
	— Workout 2 —			
	Bench Press	5	5	73%
	— Workout 1 —			
4	Squat	5	5	75%
	Deadlift	4	6	55-60%
	— Workout 2 —			
	Bench Press	5	5	75%
	— Workout 1 —			
5	Deadlift	6	4	77%
	Squat Variation	4	6	50-55%
	— Workout 2 —			
	Bench Press	6	4	78%
	— Workout 1 —			
6	Squat	6	4	77%
	Deadlift	4	6	60-65%
	— Workout 2 —			
	Paused Bench Press	6	4	78%
	— Workout 1 —			
7	Deadlift	7	3	80%
	Squat Variation	4	6	50-55%
	— Workout 2 —			
	Bench Press	6	3	80%
	— Workout 1 —			
8	Squat	8	3	80%
	Deadlift	4	6	60-65%
	— Workout 2 —			
	Paused Bench Press	6	3	80%

BASE WORK

WEEK	MAIN LIFTS	SETS	REPS	% MAX
	— Workout 3 —			
1	Squat	5	10	50%
	Deadlift	-	-	-
	— Workout 4 —			
	Bench Press	5	10	50%
	— Workout 3 —			
2	Squat	5	10	55%
	Deadlift	-	-	-
	— Workout 4 —			
	Bench Press	5	10	53%
	— Workout 3 —			
3	Squat	5	8	60%
	Deadlift	-	-	-
	— Workout 4 —			
	Bench Press	5	10	55%
	— Workout 3 —			
4	Squat	5	5	60-65%
	Deadlift Variation	4	6	55-60%
	— Workout 4 —			
	Bench Press	5	8	58%
	— Workout 3 —			
5	Squat	5	5	60-65%
	Deadlift Variation	4	6	55-60%
	— Workout 4 —			
	Bench Press	5	8	60%
	— Workout 3 —			
6	Squat	5	5	60-65%
	Deadlift Variation	4	6	55-60%
	— Workout 4 —			
	Paused Bench Press	5	5	60%
	— Workout 3 —			
7	Squat	5	5	60-65%
	Deadlift Variation	4	5	60-65%
	— Workout 4 —			
	Paused Bench Press	5	5	60-65%
	— Workout 3 —			
8	Squat	5	5	65%
	Deadlift Variation	4	5	60-65%
	— Workout 4 —			
	Paused Bench Press	5	5	60-65%

STRENGTH WORK

Week	Main Lifts	Sets	Reps	% Max
9	— Workout 1 —			
	Deadlift	6	2	85%
	Squat Variation	4	6	50-55%
	— Workout 2 —			
	Bench Press	5	3	83%
10	— Workout 1 —			
	Squat	6	2	85%
	Deadlift	4	6	60-65%
	— Workout 2 —			
	Bench Press	5	2	85%
11	— Workout 1 —			
	Deadlift	5	2	87%
	Squat Variation	4	5	55-60%
	— Workout 2 —			
	Bench Press	5	2	87%
12	— Workout 1 —			
	Squat	5	2	87%
	Deadlift	4	5	65-70%
	— Workout 2 —			
	Bench Press	5	1-2	90%
13	— Workout 1 —			
	Squat Variation	5	5	70-75%
	Deadlift Variation	4	5	70-75%
	— Workout 2 —			
	Paused Bench Press	5	5	70-75%
14	— Workout 1 —			
	*Deadlift	5-10	1	*90% +
	Squat	4	5	55-60%
	— Workout 2 —			
	Paused Bench Press	6	3	80%
15	— Workout 1 —			
	*Squat	5-10	1	*90% +
	Deadlift	4	5	65-70%
	— Workout 2 —			
	*Pause Bench Press	5-10	1	*90% +
16	— Workout 1 —			
	Squat	5	3	50%
	Deadlift	5	1	50%
	— Workout 2 —			
	Paused Bench Press	5	3	50%

BASE WORK

Week	Main Lifts	Sets	Reps	% Max
9	— Workout 3 —			
	Squat	5	5	65-70%
	Deadlift Variation	4	5	60-65%
	— Workout 4 —			
	Paused Bench Press	5	5	60-65%
10	— Workout 3 —			
	Squat	5	5	65-70%
	Deadlift Variation	4	5	65-70%
	— Workout 4 —			
	Paused Bench Press	5	5	65%
11	— Workout 3 —			
	Squat	5	5	65-70%
	Deadlift Variation	4	5	65-70%
	— Workout 4 —			
	Paused Bench Press	5	5	65-70%
12	— Workout 3 —			
	Squat	5	5	65-70%
	Deadlift Variation	4	5	65-70%
	— Workout 4 —			
	Paused Bench Press	5	5	65-70%
13	— Workout 3 —			
	Squat	5	8	60-65%
	Deadlift	-	-	-
	— Workout 4 —			
	Bench Press	5	8	60-65%
14	— Workout 3 —			
	Squat	5	5	60%
	Deadlift	5	3	65%
	— Workout 4 —			
	Paused Bench Press	5	5	65%
15	— Workout 3 —			
	Squat	5	5	65%
	Deadlift	8	1	60%
	— Workout 4 —			
	Paused Bench Press	5	5	70%
16	**Max Day**			
	Squat		**Max**	
	Bench Press		**Max**	
	Deadlift		**Max**	

*Weeks 14 & 15 - Use your competition opener for all 5-10 sets. Usually something you can do 2-3 reps with.

- **Weeks 1-4 and 13 (Workouts 1 & 2)** - AMRAP the last set of your main lift using the same working weight. AMRAP = As Many Reps As Possible *(always leave 1-2 reps in the tank and do not pause any reps).*

- **Weeks 5-12 (Workouts 1 & 2)** - Work up to a Daily Max of 1-3 reps after all your main lift sets are complete. Work up slowly taking as many sets as needed, but do not reach failure. Just move something heavy. If the weights did not move well during your sets, then just do an AMRAP for your last set with your working weight instead.

- **DO NOT change your weights after achieving a new max during the program** - Depending on your experience level, you may very well surpass your old max when doing your daily maxes. This is expected and accounted for in the programming. Do not change anything.

- **Always AMRAP the last set of Squats and Bench Press for Base Work** - DO NOT pause rep your Bench Press AMRAP sets.

- **Weeks 14 & 15** - DO NOT MAX OUT! Read the "Peak Week" section for details.

All percentages are based on your current max before beginning the program, not your projected max at the end.

If you do not know your max, then do a low estimate. As in, something you know you can do 2-3 good reps with at the start of the program. You will actually get more out of the program if you go a little lighter than you need too versus going a bit too heavy.

#MathiasMethod #FullPower

Follow @MathiasMethod on Social Media
and tag us in your #FullPower workout clips!

Also, feel free to reach out anytime with your questions
or technique checks!

WORKOUT 1 - SQUAT/DEADLIFT STRENGTH WORK

Warm-Up:

The Daily 30	1-3 Rounds
Weighted Pull-Ups	- x 25 total
Box Jumps (optional)	3-5 x 3

Technique Work:

Pause Squat / Deadlift (<50%)	3 x 5

Main Lifts:

Squat / Deadlift	See Program Chart
*Overload Set	See Program Chart Notes
Accessory Squat / Deadlift	See Program Chart

Accessory Work:

Leg Press / Glute-Ham Raises	5-10 x 10-15
Dumbbell Rows	5 x 6-8
Hammer Curls	4 x 8-10
Side Planks	3 x 30-45 sec.
Mobility Work	10+ min.

*Done after your main work is complete, and never to failure.

Go to MathiasMethod.com for in-depth exercise descriptions.

Workout 2 - Bench Press Strength Work

Warm-Up:

The Daily 30	1-3 Rounds
Lat Machine / Cable Rows	3-5 x 10

Technique Work:

Pause Bench Press (<50%)	3 x 5

Main Lift:

Bench Press	See Program Chart
*Overload Set	See Program Chart Notes

Accessory Work:

Dumbbell Press / Incline Dumbbell Press	5-10 x 6-10
Military Press / Dumbbell Military Press	5 x 5-10
Triceps Press Downs	5-10 x 10-15
Face Pulls	5-10 x 10-15
Hanging Leg Raises / Weighted Crunches	5 x 5-10
Mobility Work	10+ min.

*Done after your main work is complete, and <u>never to failure</u>.

Go to MathiasMethod.com for in-depth exercise descriptions.

WORKOUT 3 - SQUAT/DEADLIFT BASE WORK

Warm-Up:

The Daily 30	1-3 Rounds
Pull-Ups	- x 30-50

Technique Work:

Pause Squat (<50%)	3 x 5

Main Lifts:

Squat	See Program Chart
Deadlift Variation	See Program Chart

Accessory Work:

Leg Curls	5 x 10-15
Lat Pull-Downs / Seated Cable Rows	5 x 10-15
Dumbbell Curls	3 x 10-15
Weighted Planks	3 x 30-60 sec.
Mobility Work	10+ min.

Go to MathiasMethod.com for in-depth exercise descriptions.

WORKOUT 4 - BENCH PRESS BASE WORK

Warm-Up:

The Daily 30	1-3 Rounds
Face Pulls	3-5 x 10-15

Technique Work:

Pause Bench Press (<50%)	3 x 5

Main Lift:

Bench Press	See Program Chart

Accessory Work:

Incline Dumbbell Press	5 x 10-15
Dumbbell Military Press	5 x 10-15
Triceps Skull Crushers	5-10 x 10-15
Reverse Flyes	4 x 10-15
Lateral Raises	4 x 10-15
Leg Raises / Crunches	5 x 10-15
Mobility Work	10+ min.

Go to MathiasMethod.com for in-depth exercise descriptions.

All workouts and training protocols follow the Mathias Method Strength Principles.

In the Mathias Method Strength System we don't train muscle groups. We train movements and base our workouts on improving one lift. This is because lifts like the squat, bench press, and deadlift are all full body lifts. They take your entire body working in unison to perfect and do not target one specific area.

By building up these powerful compound movements we will develop strength and muscle throughout our entire body.

We also believe in using only the most effective accessory exercises. Big bang exercises that build big muscle and big strength. Yeah, they are hard ones and they make you brutally strong too.

This training style may be different than what you are used to, but it is what has worked for me and countless others with the same goal of getting brutally strong.

The details of your training are discussed next.

THE WARM-UP

Warm-ups are just what you think. They are simply meant too, warm-up your body for the intense work ahead, but not overly fatigue you.

If you are not used to doing some warm-up exercises before your main work, then it will be fatiguing at first until your body gets more conditioned. This is part of developing the work capacity to lift heavy weight, so do not skip this just because you do not feel like it. If you want to get stronger, you're gonna have to put in the work no matter how you "feel".

Warm-ups should be relatively easy and never done to failure.

Every workout you do should start with 1-3 rounds of *The Daily 30* (see page 4) to practice your movement patterns and improve mobility while you warm-up. This may seem unnecessary, but it will do wonders for your strength and help to alleviate any muscle or joint pain you have.

SQUAT / DEADLIFT WARM-UP EXERCISES

For Squat/Deadlift Workouts you will also warm-up with pull-ups. Back strength is one of the most important factors in providing strength for all of your lifts, which is why we have you start every workout with a pulling exercise.

If you can't do pull ups, then you can use a band for assistance or replace these with heavy lat pull-downs. However, if you've been training for a while you know that there really is no replacement for pull-ups. They are a vital exercise that our bodies were designed to do and need to be practiced often. They decompress your spine and build back strength like nothing else can!

You can do these with your hands facing in (chin-ups - bicep focused) or facing away (pull-ups - Lat focused) as you desire.

Do as many sets as it takes to get to the set number of reps, never going to failure.

For weighted pull-ups you want to aim for a weight that allows you to do 5 sets of 5 reps or so. Adjust the weight as needed.

If you cannot do 10 pull-ups in a row, then either do heavy lat pull-downs for 5x10 on your Base Work training days or cut the reps down to 30 total for those workouts.

Also, as part of your warm-up on Squat/Deadlift Strength Work days you can include plyometrics. This is optional, but highly recommended.

Plyometrics have an incredible ability to prepare your body for maximal lifts through the reflexive contraction that they provide, very similar to a maximal squat or deadlift. The key is to jump to a difficult height onto a box, but not so high that you risk missing the box. Then slowly over time try to increase the height. As the box height increases, so too will your strength!

BENCH PRESS WARM-UP EXERCISES

For both Bench Press Workouts your first warm-up exercise will be a pulling exercise to help counteract all the pressing you are about to do.

Choose any back exercise that you feel helps you keep your shoulders healthy and back strong. It is best to do a horizontal row versus something like a cable pull-down, because of the angle of pull mimicking a bench press. Keep the weight moderate and really warm-up your back.

For added strength and performance follow my *How To Warm-Up Guide* (see page 4) before every workout!

TECHNIQUE WORK

Exercise Technique is a crucial part of any movement based training program. Without proper technique your body will learn improper movement patterns that can hold back your strength and cause injury.

Technique is so important that it should be checked and improved every time you start a training session!

Your technique work is still part of your warm-up and therefore only light weights (<50% of your maximum) should be used to prevent over fatiguing yourself. The focus is on improving your movement pattern by utilizing perfect form, under controlled movements.

The main goals of this exercise is to prepare your body for the more intense work ahead, build up weaknesses and increase work capacity.

When squats are your main lift for the workout, your technique work will be pause squats where you pause at the bottom position for 1-2 seconds before exploding back up to build more strength in the bottom position.

When deadlifts are your main lift, your technique work will be either your normal deadlift variation, or a 1 inch deficit deadlift if you need to build more strength off the floor.

For bench press workouts, your main lift will always be paused bench press. This will help you get used to pausing for competition and help build more strength at the bottom of the lift.

For these exercises, you will only do 3 sets of 5 perfect reps. Again, the goals are to improve the motion of this exercise and better prepare your body for the work ahead, not to pre-fatigue those muscles.

After completing your Technique Work, you are ready to begin your workout!

Start with your first exercise by doing the same number of repetitions you plan to train with for that day. If you are doing 3 reps for your working sets, do all your warm-ups with 3 reps. Start with a low intensity and work your way up slowly.

If you want to learn how to perfect your lifting technique, plus the best accessory exercises to build them up, get my in-depth squat, bench and deadlift technique guides (see page 4).

THE MAIN LIFT

The main lift, or main lifts, of any given workout, is the focus point of the session, where you put in the most effort. All of the training before and after the main lift is set to better improve this movement.

This program's Main Lifts are the squat, bench press and deadlift, in which squat and deadlift will rotate focus every week, while bench press remains constant. One day per week your main lift will be done at a high intensity with low reps to build maximal strength, and on another day they will be done with a light-moderate intensity as you accumulate volume and practice technique, creating a higher potential for strength gain.

Together, varying between light, moderate and heavy loads will allow for continuous growth without stagnation.

Follow the 16-Week Program Chart for your main lift sets, reps and intensity.

Always warm-up to your working weight slowly during each workout to fully prepare yourself for the work ahead.

OVERLOAD SETS

Overload sets are part of your Main Lift work on Strength Work training days. For this you will either do an AMRAP (as many reps as possible) set or work up to a Daily Max.

AMRAP

Weeks 1-4 and 13 - AMRAP the last set of your Main Lift using the same working weight.

For your AMRAP sets, do as many reps as possible minus one. We always minus one because we do not want to ever risk failure. It is better to save some for later, then grind with bad form or risk missing a lift, which stalls progress.

DAILY MAX

Weeks 5-12 - Work up to a Daily Max of 1-3 reps after all your main sets are done.

A Daily Max is a near maximum lift for that given day. It is not a true maximum, because you are fatigued from all the previous work.

For your Daily Max, work up to something heavy, but do not push so hard that you lose technique or risk failure.

Depending on your experience level, you may very well surpass your old max when doing your daily maxes. This is expected and accounted for in the programming. Do not change anything.

DO NOT do any overload sets on weeks 14-16!

MAIN ACCESSORY WORK

Your main accessory is the main accessory lift that directly helps improve your main lift. The idea for this lift is not to overly fatigue you beyond recovery, but rather just hit your muscles from a different angle to stimulate new growth. Just get in some work and do not push too hard. You already did your main strength work. So, just work the motion with moderate weight and then move on.

This lift is included for all Squat/Deadlift Workouts. For squats your main accessory is the deadlift and for deadlifts it is the squat.

In any program, you can't talk about squats without talking about deadlifts, and you can't talk about deadlift without talking about squats. These two lifts work hand in hand to benefit each other. That is why we programmed for both lifts twice per week.

For your main accessory, you can do any variation of the lift that best helps to improve your strength. This can vary every workout or stay the same. However, it is best to do a variation that helps to bring up a weakness.

- **For Squats**, if you have weak quads you should do close stance squats or front squats. If you have weak hips or hamstrings, then do wide stance squats or box squats.

- **For Deadlifts**, you should do 1-2 inch deficit deadlifts using a conventional stance, even if you normally do Sumo.

- **Bench Press has no main accessory.** However, you can modify your Base Work Main Lift to be a Bench Press variation in order to correct a weakness.

For example, if you have weak triceps you can do closegrip bench press. If you have weak shoulders and chest, then you can do incline bench press. Just make sure that you adjust the weights based on that variation's max. As in, if you are doing incline bench press instead of pause bench, base the weight on your incline bench press max, not your pause bench max.

ACCESSORY WORK

Your accessory work is just a few hard hitting exercises to help build more strength and muscle throughout your entire body. You will be pretty exhausted by this point, but push through and take it as a mental challenge that will make you even stronger.

Your accessory work should be performed with moderate-intensity to allow for optimal muscle growth and proper technique. Always maintain good form to ensure proper muscle activation throughout the entire lift.

Focus on stimulating the muscle rather than just throwing around tremendous weight. It is important to always be in control of the weight.

Work every exercise hard and try to move up in weight when you can.

Make sure to finish off every workout with some mobility work to prevent injury.

Squat / Deadlift Accessory Work

Your Squat focused Strength Work will have leg press as your first accessory exercise after deadlifts. Do 5-10 hard sets with moderate to heavy weight and really push your legs to build as much quad strength as possible. If you do not have a leg press, then you can do front squats instead.

Your Deadlift focused Strength Work will have glute-ham raises as your first accessory exercise. This is one of the most effective exercises for building brutally strong hamstrings that can support huge lifts. If you cannot perform these properly I recommend you start with controlled negative reps (lower yourself slowly) until you build the strength to do reps on your own.

You can start by kneeling on a pad and having a friend sit on your ankles and descend slowly under control before doing a push up to press yourself back up. When you get strong enough to do these without assistance, your lifts will likely have shot up significantly by now and you can start holding a weight plate across your chest.

If you do not have a gute-ham raise at your gym, or a friend to help out, you can just do some heavy leg curls instead, but it just won't give you the same results.

Next you will move onto heavy dumbbell rows. Feel free to use straps on these in order to grip heavier weight, but only go as heavy as you can while maintaining proper form. Then pick any bicep curl variation you like before moving onto some side planks and finishing with some mobility work to keep your body injury free.

For your Base Work accessories you start off with leg curls to counter balance all the quad work you just got from volume squats. Then pick any back exercises you want before moving onto some curls and weighted planks.

If you are having knee pain it is likely due to your quads overpowering your hamstrings so do some light leg curls at the start of your workouts for extra accessory work to build up your hamstring strength.

BENCH PRESS ACCESSORY WORK

The accessory work for your Bench Press Strength Work starts off with dumbbell press, or incline dumbbell press if you have weak shoulders. This is one of the best bench press accessory exercises you can do, because it mimics the bench press with more freedom of movement and helps to build up your stabilizing muscles. Plus, you can change the angle of your hands to target different muscles and even increase the range of motion by letting your hands drop slightly lower than your chest.

Do 5-10 hard sets with moderate to heavy weight and really push yourself to build as much upper body strength as possible. Then do the same for your shoulders with Military Press.

After doing all that pressing work it will be time to target the most important muscle to increase your bench press…your triceps! You will do cable press downs to build both big and strong triceps ready to press BIG weight with ease. You have already done a ton of heavy tricep work with all your presses so this is a relatively easy triceps exercise to help finish them off for the day. Go moderately heavy and make sure you feel your triceps giving out before you move on to the next exercise.

Next up is face pulls. These are great for building your rear delts and upper back, counteracting all the pressing work you just did. These are very important for your shoulder health and need to be pushed hard. Put everything you have left into these to get your shoulders set back in place.

How many sets you do out of the 5-10 given for most of these exercises greatly depends on your your experience level and how much volume your muscles can tolerate. So, let your muscles be the judge, stopping only when they start to give out. If you are a newer lifter, 5 sets may be enough. If you are already a pretty big bencher, you may need all 10 sets. Just go until you feel it is time to move on.

Finish with some heavy ab work and mobility to keep your body looking and feeling good.

For your Base Work accessories you will be doing a ton of dumbbell work to make sure both of your arms are getting built up equally. Dumbbells are very versatile and can help to hit your muscles from different angles while making your stabilizers work extra hard. This is extremely important for being able to bench BIG weight.

CARDIO/CONDITIONING

Conditioning, or cardio, is not necessary for this program, but can assist with dropping weight and improving recovery, if needed. Just DO NOT do cardio to warm-up!

Conditioning, is any form of work that improves your cardiovascular health and total work capacity while assisting with the goals of training. Some examples of conditioning are; jogging, sprints, jump rope, battle ropes, light circuit training, a daily WOD, sled dragging, or just manual labor.

Conditioning is meant to increase the ability for your body to withstand work and become stronger. If you have low cardiovascular health and little muscular endurance then the amount of work your body can withstand is greatly diminished, along with your ability to become stronger. So, if you have a low work capacity, you should add in conditioning until it improves.

Conditioning can be performed 2-4 times per week for 10-20 minutes at a time. You may utilize high intensity interval training (HIIT) or moderate intensity steady state training.

With high intensity intervals, work to rest should be at a 1:1 or 1:2 ratio. For moderate intensity steady state conditioning, the body should stay in motion throughout the entire time with little to no resistance in order to sustain a raised heart rate during the time used.

It is best to do conditioning immediately after all accessory work, just before mobility work. This will add to the work already done in the workout and allow for the greatest increase in muscular advancement.

Conditioning can also be done on non-training days if preferred, but should then be done for 20-30 minutes. Remember, conditioning is meant to condition your body, not break it down beyond what your body can repair before the next training session. Use relatively light loads and just keep moving.

Mobility Work

Mobility Work is 10+ minutes of stretching at the end of every workout used increase flexibility, prevent injury and improve recovery. Focus on stretching out the muscle you just worked, or other tight areas.

It can be as simple as doing just 2-3 stretches for 2 minutes each to fix your elbow, shoulder, ankle, or hip pain.

Mobility work can also be replaced by yoga or any other activity that improves your body's ability to move as intended without pain, such as rolling out soft tissues.

It is best to mobilize right after a workout, but it can also be done on non-training days.

The goal is to get at least 30-40 minutes of mobilization done weekly to enhance your recovery and performance. That is just 10 minutes 3-4 times per week.

Check out my Mobility Exercises on MathiasMethod.com!

Rest Periods

Rest periods between sets will vary for each part of the workout.

During your warm-up you can superset all your exercises together, as the intensity is not very high for these exercises. Or you can take your time with each exercise to prevent fatiguing yourself too much before your main work. It is your warm-up, so do what works best for you.

For all your Main Lifts, rest as long as you need between sets, but realize that the longer you take between sets, the longer the workout will last from all the sets you have to do.

Typically rest should be 2-3 minutes for loads less than 75% of your maximum and 3-5 minutes for anything heavier. You can take longer if needed, but don't waste all your time waiting to be ready. It is supposed to be hard and tiring, so push yourself and improve your conditioning if needed.

For all accessory work, rest 1-2 minutes between sets.

TRAINING TO FAILURE

There are 2 types of failure in training; technical and absolute.

- **Technical failure** is the point in which you can no longer perform a repetition with reasonably perfect technique. This commonly occurs 1-2 repetitions before absolute failure.

- **Absolute failure** is when no more repetitions can be completed without assistance.

It is good to know what failure feels like, but most of your work should be done with reasonably perfect technique to build the most optimal amount of strength.

You should really only reach technical failure on the last 1-2 sets of any workout, if at all. This means you reached maximal stimuli of the muscle fibers and central nervous system while still performing safe technique.

Reaching absolute failure too often will result in a much greater chance for injury and a much longer recovery period that may extend beyond the next training session. Not only that, but it teaches improper lifting technique as your body fights to lift the weight, and makes you weaker in the long run.

If you are training to failure, then you are training to fail!

The idea for strength training is too, accumulate volume for growth over multiple training sessions per week utilizing perfect practice. This will ensure safety while gaining the most amount of strength over time.

IF YOU DO FAIL

In training, your main lifts should never go beyond technical failure during this entire program. However, if you ever do fail a rep, then drop the weight by 10% multiplied by the number of reps you have left in your set and do the rest of your sets in shame.

For example, if you failed your last rep, then take off only 10%. If you failed on your 4th rep out of 5, then take off 20%.

If you complete the rest of your sets at this new weight with good form, then you can go back up in weight, but this decreased percentage is your punishment for not recovering properly. Shame on you! Just don't blame me for your lack of preparation.

Also, if the weight is effecting your technique too much and you are moving slow or out of position, then drop the weight by 10-20% until it looks better. It is your job to lift the weight properly and if you cannot do that, then your punishment is lifting lighter weight until you can get it right.

Again, not my fault. Just do it right and make it look easy!

FINAL NOTES

- Recovery is the most important thing! It doesn't matter what you do in the gym; if you can't recover from it, then you are not going to progress. Recovery is the only thing that is going to hold you back from making this program a success. So make sure you are getting enough sleep and fuel! That part is on you.

- As you get stronger throughout the program, your working weights will feel easier, and you will likely surpass your current maxes multiple times when going for your Daily Max attempts. Still, make sure you base the Program Chart percentages on your previous max at the start of the program. Not your new weekly maxes.

- Make sure you are doing your *Daily 30* to help with recovery and mobility throughout the entire program.

- Be sure to practice your lifts exactly how they are supposed to be performed in the competition. That means practicing holding deadlifts at the top and pausing bench presses as you get closer to the competition.

- If you have any concerns about your squat, bench press or deadlift technique, and whether they will pass judging at a powerlifting meet, then I highly recommend you get my in-depth technique guides which cover exactly what judges consider a "good lift". *See next page.*

- Email me (ryan@mathiasmethod.com) with any questions!

- One more thing…

WOULD YOU DO ME A FAVOR?

Thank you for reading and I hope you learned a lot!

Before you go, please do me a HUGE favor and take a moment to let me know what you liked most about this book by leaving a review on Amazon! I read all my reviews and I love hearing how my work has helped others.

Plus, it helps more people learn what they can get from this book!

If you were not completely satisfied with the content of this book please let me know by emailing me directly and I will be happy to answer your questions or help you further.

Thank you, and keep getting stronger my friends!

Email: ryan@mathiasmethod.com

Do you know someone that would benefit from this book?

Please tell them about it!

Everyone can benefit from getting stronger!

MORE BOOKS BY RYAN J. MATHIAS

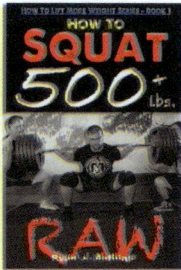

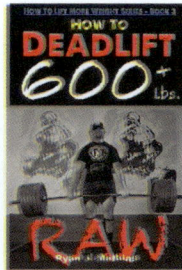

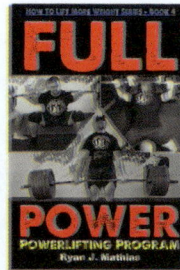

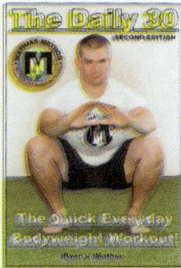

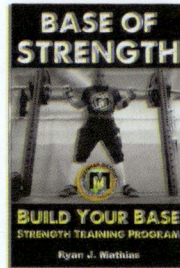

Follow The Strength Blog

We have over 200+ articles on how to get stronger and workout properly, in and out of the gym!

Go to MathiasMethod.com to follow the Strength Blog and get all the awesome NEW Content we put out!

- **New Articles**

- **Workout Programs**

- **Valuable Strength Training Resources!**

FOLLOW US ON SOCIAL MEDIA

Facebook: @MathiasMethodStrength

Instagram: @MathiasMethod

Twitter: @MathiasMethod

YouTube: @MathiasMethodStrength

Reddit: u/mathiasmethod

STRENGTH
STRENGTHWORLD.STORE
WORLD

Ironworks Gym

153 South Auburn St.
Grass Valley, CA 95945

PHONE #: (530) 272-9462

Home of the Mathias Method STRENGTH WARRIORS!

Thank you for allowing us to use your awesome facility to help make the world a stronger place!

Strength is only the beginning.

It is what you do with it next that really matters.

Printed in Great Britain
by Amazon

24883395R00030